Jesus
Feeds a Crowd

Bibleworld Books contains stories adapted
from the *Contemporary English Version* of the Bible.
Each book is designed to provide early readers with a text
adapted from Scripture in a form and manner that helps them
develop their reading skills and introduce them to the narrative of the Bible.

Adapted from:
Mission Literacy Readers Level 1 & 2
© 2008 American Bible Society
Used by permission.

Jesus Feeds a Crowd is based on Matthew 14:13-21

ISBN: 978-0-901518-74-3

Series 1: Book 3

Illustrated by Graeme Hewitson

© 2017 The Scottish Bible Society (Formerly The National Bible Society of Scotland).
Company number SC238687, Scottish Charity SC010767
All rights reserved.

The Scottish Bible Society
7 Hampton Terrace, Edinburgh. EH12 5XU
www.scottishbiblesociety.org

Series 1: Who was Jesus

Jesus and the Storm
Jesus Heals a Man
Jesus Feeds a Crowd
Jesus Walks on the Water

Bibleworld Books provides three full session outlines to accompany each story book with games and activities designed to raise each child's learning potential.

Available for free download at www.bibleworld.co.uk

One day, Jesus went across Lake Galilee with his disciples, so they could be alone.

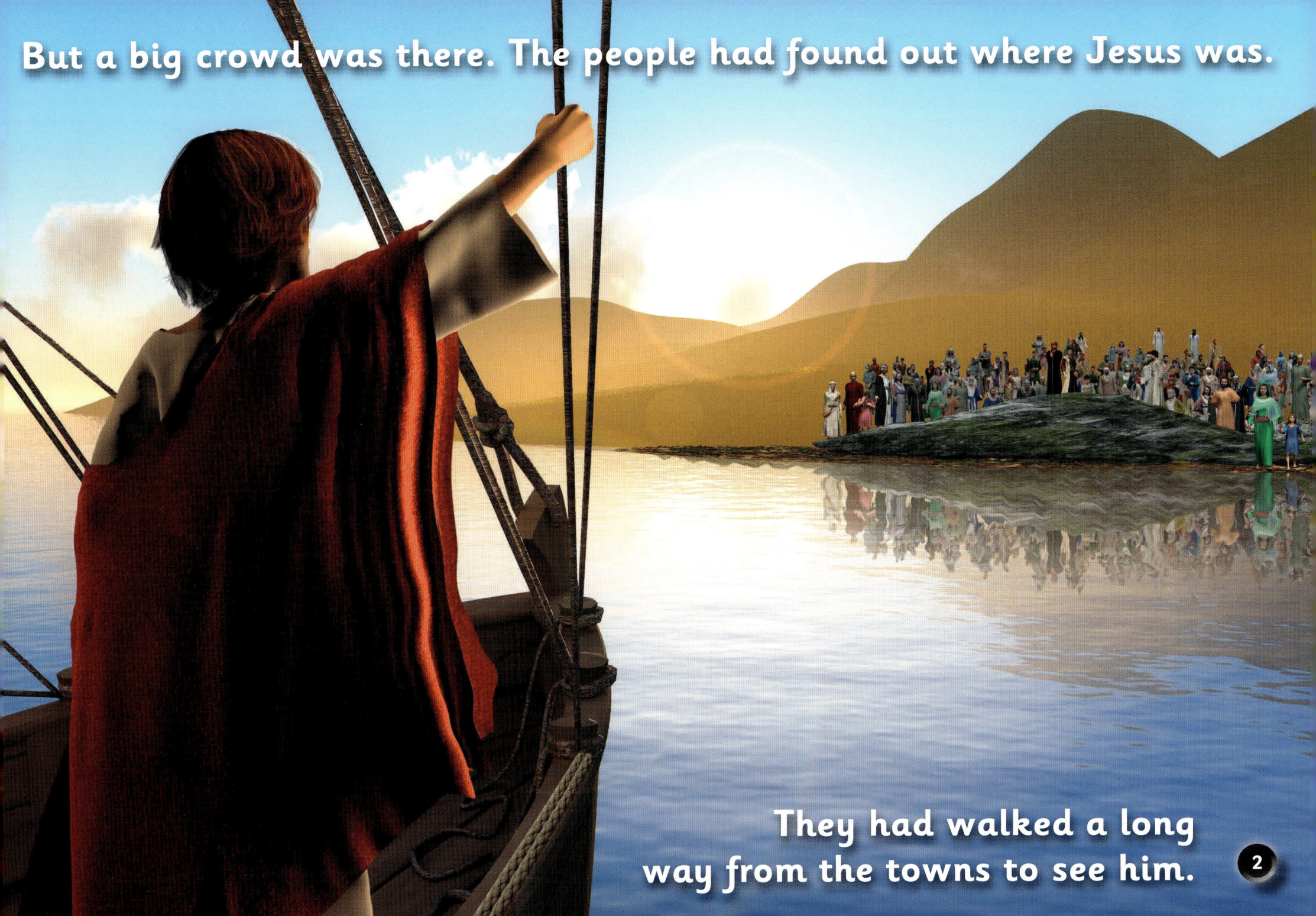

But a big crowd was there. The people had found out where Jesus was.

They had walked a long way from the towns to see him.

So Jesus spent all day healing them.

Late in the day, his disciples came to him.

"It's getting late," they said, "and this place is like a desert. The people need to leave to buy food."

"No," Jesus said, "they can stay."
"You can give them food."

The men were surprised. They stared at him,

and said, "But all we have is five loaves of bread and two fish!"

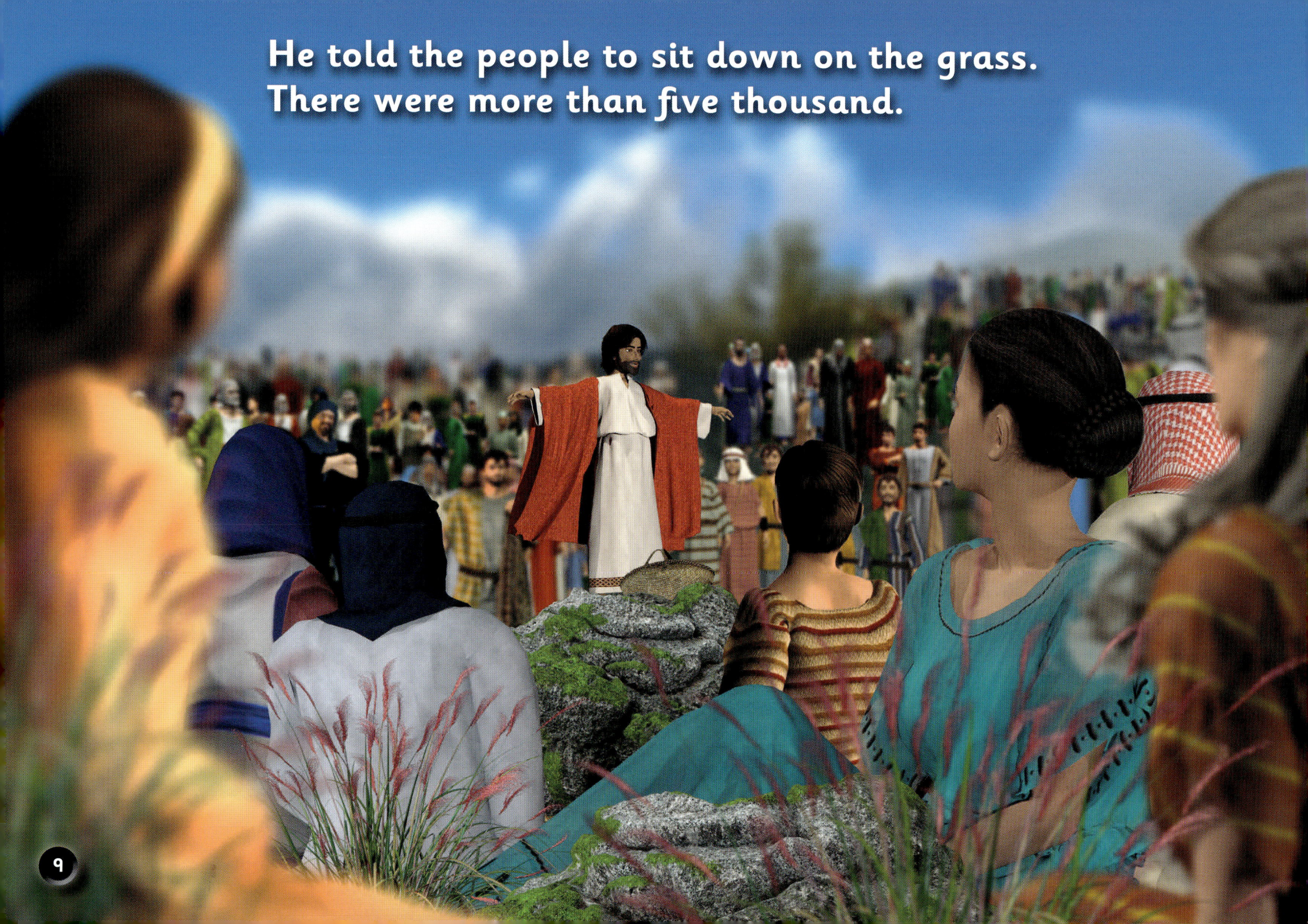
He told the people to sit down on the grass. There were more than five thousand.

Jesus took the bread and the fish.

He broke the loaves of bread,

and handed the food back to his disciples.

Then the disciples gave the food to the people.

"It won't be enough!" they were thinking. But they were wrong.

It *was* enough!

The people ate all they wanted, and there was still more.

The disciples picked up the leftovers.